Thanks, Sharon Ann —
I will enjoy this book.

2001 25th

It's early Christmas day - dark outside - the boys are fast asleep in the back bedroom at Homesite - Marie won't even peep for another hour or two - and that makes me in charge of the homestead. We made "rather merry" last nite and as usual the boys inundated Mom and I with gifts; The stockings were full, the living room was full and when I come home, I had to sit down and list all my loot lest I forget to say Thanks to all the givers.

Helen couldn't join us this year. She has been extremely ill for some time now. The boys went to see her yesterday and take her her gifts. For some reason, Mom just can't bring herself to see her but we will go up today if nothing happens. It's the first Xmas I can ever remember that Helen didn't come by and give us our presents and open her birthday gift. Something inside breaks when traditions are broken.

#

Sitting around waiting for Ruby to arrive home.
She has my cell just in case and I promised to
hang around in case of car trouble. The
boys are planning to do something but don't
know what. I think they are just content to
loll around. The sun is brightly shining
and its a beautiful day.

Two + years later — June 2004 5th
Saturday

I found my book in my stationery
drawer and looked at the empty
pages, wishing that I had filled
it with memories of the last
2½ years — most of which I will
not be able to recall.

Today finds Homesite quiet.
Marie seems to be perking right
along after falling and fracturing
her shoulder the first of March.
She was in a lot of pain. "I don't
want to endure another month
like that one!"

Our great sadness right now
is Helen's condition. Early in
the year she fell and hit her
head wounding her eye severely
and this past week has again
fallen and broken her lip while
visiting Kim, Rita's daughter, in
Hemet. So, there she lies today
in a hospital in Hemet.
Our hearts hurt.

October 31st, 2004
Halloween

the last day of October (a Sunday) was
a beautiful day; Sunny, light breeze
and all. Rube and I breakfasted
at carson's and shopped a little.
When I arrived home, Marie wanted
to go to the store for some treats
for her RummyKub tomorrow — just
Grace and she. Bernice passed
away last year and Helen is
still unable to get up.

Then this evening I
passed out the Trick-or-Treat
candy — Believe it or not —
there were only three (3)
who came to the door
this year. So we have a
lot of leftover candy,

One more day 'til election
thank Goodness, Bush & Kerry
are neck in neck. I can
only pray that our nation will
extract itself from this mess
in Iraq — I think Bush is in
over his head so I hope Kerry
is up to it — I guess we'll see.

20 June 2006 Tue

not just the days but the years are passing so swiftly. I turned 72 in April — how sobering — and yet, not sad.

I am still at the homestead in my room/studio — — — still making do — — — still trying to keep myself occupied. Rube and I have been going to Bethany Assembly for a year and a half and know about a dozen people by now. We often try to understand why that is.

The boys just went home on Friday after a 2 week stay. Rube and ~~I went~~ to ~~Laughlin~~ for 4 days and to Victor Valley — did a lot of shopping although the temp was above 100 every day — but we did have good food.

I had a stress test yesterday and an echo cardiogram a couple of weeks ago and was diagnosed w/ MVP. I have a prescription for Topral. I'll just have to wait and see.

"Life" goes on.

- November 2006 — Marie to Hospital
- January 2007 — 5th to 23rd Hospital (911)
- April 15, 2007 — 18th Hospitals
  (911) Paradise Vally to Sharp Coronado

○ June 24, 2007   11:30 AM

I am sad beyond belief.
Mom left.
I could not stop it — nor
would I if I could.

I really can't talk about
it now with any clarity

Glen Abby handled the service
Viewing was June 26 Tuesday
Graveside was on Wednesday 27th
— those who loved her came
and I tried to remember
to hold a mein that
would please her.